The Invisibles

05-10-06

The Invisibles

A Collection of Poetry & Artwork

Writer & Artist: Donia Gobar, MD, MPH

iUniverse, Inc.

New York Lincoln Shanghai

The Invisibles
A Collection of Poetry & Artwork

iUniverse, Inc.

For information address:
iUniverse, Inc.
2021 Pine Lake Road, Suite 100
Lincoln, NE 68512
www.iuniverse.com

Front cover design, layout, and painting by Donia Gobar (author)
Back cover: design and layout by Donia Gobar (author)
(author's photos, book description, short biography)

ISBN: 0-595-29303-4 (pbk)
ISBN: 0-595-75026-5 (cloth)

Printed in the United States of America

Dedicated
To
The Innocent People of the World

Contents
List of Poems

Contents—List of Paintings

(originals are all in color and of larger sizes)

Front cover (36"X28" acrylic*)—Listen…Oh Watch…

> Note*: In creation of this painting, the artist (author) was inspired by the picture of "Afghan Girl" photographed by Steve McCurry.

Acknowledgement

My deepest gratitude to my parents, whose wisdom and life examples have been, and always will be, my guiding light.

I am grateful to my daughter Carrie (Afsana), my "kindred spirit," whose personality and outlook contribute to humanity and bring joy to my life.

My sincere appreciation for the guidance, love, and friendship of my family and those whom I love dearly, whose existences enrich and beautify the world.

I am thankful to Nate Mayer, a young and gifted individual, for his technical assistance and skillful photography in preparation of the artwork included in this book.

My sincere thanks to Rifka Keilson and Valerie Haas, the iUniverse, Inc., Publishing Service representatives, for their support and guidance during the manuscript submission process.

I am impressed by the professionalism of the expert editors at iUniverse, and am truly grateful for their recognition and review of my work.

Finally, I thank iUniverse, Inc. for giving me the chance to dedicate my writing and artwork to the innocent people of the world.

Donia Gobar
dgobard@yahoo.com

Humanity survives through wisdom, courage, and justice.
Violence is *never* the answer to problems of the world.
And, truth—*the unconditional truth*, is the key to humanity.

—*Donia Gobar*

Regardless of *who*, *where*, and *when*, *we all* are responsible for the path that humanity takes, *and* for what the *history of humanity* will hold for its future generations.

—*Donia Gobar*

Afternoon Nap

On a green, shimmering summer day
the little boy tiptoed out with a silent pray;
that his mother in deep sleep may stay,
and he, from his needed nap, could get away.

The smell of grass and roses all around.
The weeping willows shadowed the ground,
as their soft emerald hair touched the ground.
The boy became a whisper in summer sound.

The heated earth burned his naked feet,
running, barely touching the baking street.
Gasping, he reached the shaded retreat,
beside the joyful, singing, sheltered creek.

The cool bank embraced his tiny chest.
On the old oak a little bird chirped in a nest.
The tadpole gang rushed on their quest.
On the boy's face, a big smile came to rest.

A second stretched to a million years.
In his never-ending world, no tears, no fears.
His fingers made clay castles and piers.
The future became younger by a thousand years.

The gleaming summer day was fading.
The cheeky, playful squirrels were racing.

Sunset found the boy, softly breathing;
eyes shut, smiling in his hideout, dreaming.

The breeze gently ruffled his light hair.
The hero on his horse was riding unaware.
Dream rode beside him, sweet and fair;
"No afternoon nap," whispered she in his ear.

Allusion

In white shimmering nights, in dark days,
in moonlit skies, in beaming sunrays,
she was a soft raindrop, a candle's light,
a star's kiss, an angle's sight.
O night…

Her heart was the marble in life's hand;
or was it a fledgling in hunter's band?
Her mind—a clean page in thought's hand,
or was it a soft bed in storm's land?
O night, tell me!

Her gaze was speaker of children's hopes;
or was it a panorama of weeping souls?
Her fingers—pilgrims on legend's road,
or were they scribers of stories untold?
Oh, night…O mysterious dark night.

Now…her eyes—the old pilgrims of lives,
and her lips—a silent seal for victim's lives?
The falling tears—confused in stormy waves…
the world-weary pilgrim—tempered and brave…
O proud vague night.

Starlight became sparks under iron heels.
Angels' songs became shrill morbid yells.
The tranquil spring became storm, became storm…
In the lands of deserts and seas,
became floods, became flames
O creepy, dark, cold night.

Allusions

A quarter of a century—Imagine...

Imagine you were a child

woken by the loud sounds,
and screams,
as the *mother of bombs*
has shaken the grounds
and broken homes and body parts
scattered around,

and you,

watching

the disfigured body of *your mother*
laying down, on a mud floor,
and the sudden lash of pain...
"Whose leg is there?—A yard away..."

Imagine you trudge along
through ruins of a lost city...
Your bloody half-leg
dangling behind
through bits and pieces of bodies
leaving a red trail behind.

Under a misty gray sky,
all alone—a six-year-old child.
and you cry quietly,
far away...

Imagine!
The military bases

The winning hounds,
And the gloating generals,
The panicked losing troops,
And the plans for the next bombing
The bottles of vodka...
And the innocent, sacrificial solders—
whose names you may never know—
saluting, following orders...

Destroyed towns and cultures...

And the dried-up wells...

And you ask yourself,
Why?
What for?

Imagine

Ariana[1]
(Dedicated to my country of birth)

Such a sad silence…
This bottomless whirlpool of grief

O…the gasping airless senses
and the old dry tears
still burning,
still running
on dusty ruins of *Beloved Ariana*

Did I hear *Her* bitter laughter?
Did I hear *Her* whisper?

> *"I Will Never Be Gone…*
> *I will never be gone…*
> *I will never be gone…"*

---

1.   Ariana ("Aryana") is the ancient name of Afghanistan

Before the End

Nightlife Bar's green lights hiss
and slobber
over the cobalt stone sidewalks
in search of passing drunkards
and lonesome souls.

I walk in hallways lined with daunting norms
where I search for human faces
behind bleak masks.

My feet, tired and bruised
inside this misfit life,
bought and sold by those I don't even know…
Some strange strength elevates me
above my life;
and I gaze over the wreckage of my own,
while
crying for souls I don't even know…
Irony surfs on the waves of salty laughter,
crushing at the coasts I used to know.

The little girl running against the wind,
laughing,
steps into my age-colored shoes,
dancing.
Reality chuckles,
and *she* disappears in time…

Last night I found a picture of mine,
delicate figure,
dark shoulder-length waves,
a half-smile,

with brave young life in embrace,
looking down,
in a side-cast shy gaze,
her hands raised with grace
in an Eastern dance…

Now, mirror finds me—watching,
in serene silence,
the evanescent moments of fall,
and of mine.
A brave welcome, a half-smile…

A fresh breeze,
whispering aged wisdom's songs,
touches my heart—
now slightly trembling,
in the chill of time,
before winter,
before night…

Birthday

On that cold Thursday afternoon
under a dome-shaped roof
I was born in an exile land.
My mother and my father,
looking at a dusty distance,
thinking of human blossoms
and life's untimely frost,
in that exile land.

Years have passed
but
the warmth of their love has last
through life's stormy casts…
in all exile lands.

Now…they are gone forever.
Many frosts have come
and gone,
before time,
and lingering too long.
Branches have trembled in cold nights
and lovely leaves
have turned into orphans, forlorn.
Fall is pouring its sweet sadness
before dusk,
over the shimmering surface
of a lonely pond.

My tired heart is running,
losing count of time.

The child born under the dome-shaped roof
is kneeling down on God's land,
offering
all her love,
all her life,
to her mother, to her father,
in this exile land.

Birthday

Ceaseless

Across the room I saw you—among all.
Your eyes—
the shaded river in fall.
Your voice—
the words of a hero,
as rushing tides on a blue night shore,
echoed in the brave world of allure.

Time had stood still.
Distance had disappeared.
And voices had vanished—till
I could breath again,
think again…
"Who were you?"
When you held my hand
in safety of your grasping, strong hands;
my mind, hastily, had whispered,
"When will I see you—or, at all?"
I had wondered—
that night in fall.

Now, across the life borders,
my thoughts linger, rather sadly,
on the edge of distance between us—
the infinity…
And as the lonely silence weeps,
my mind whispers,
absentmindedly,
"Where is the honest grasp of your hands?"

"Where does echo
your rushing laughter's sound…?"

And the memory tides sway me
on a blue life shore—
to smile,
and to cry,
as I remember,
the first time I ever knew you
and the last time I ever saw you.

Ceaseless

Confusion

Eagles whispered to eagles,
"Look upon *MAN*, rushing along…
Meeting to meeting, day after day."

Trees trembled, shedding leaves in sorrow,
"Forms and forms, covers—covering truth,
office to office, and files to files."

Rats stayed silent in awe, while
Chairmen cleared their throats,
declared the solutions to problems,
motioned, and seconded the items in agendas.

Old janitors on night shifts,
their backs bent, walked slowly,
wiping the cigar dust off leather furniture
and carpeted floors…

Problems spread their skirts in darkness,
and "confusion"
grew in sparkles of blind lights…

Eagles circled in the sky above,
and the *child* looked up and wondered,
"*What are* the grownups doing?"

Confusion

Dance

My pounding heart
overflows
under the cascade of tears,
and
my dark eyes
drown
in foggy memories…

In Blue Danube's trance,
hazily,
sad melodies,
and warm bodies
sleep,
and old shadows
creep…

My weathered soul soars
over faraway oceans,
and
we dance with Strauss
in the arms of centuries…

On a hot summer night,
lazily,
the small towns
sleep…

Do You Know Me?

I am in cold broken houses
On sizzling country roads
In dark alleys of glorious cities
In hospital corridors
On the steps of forgotten shacks
In the age of electronics…

I am there—where you live.

I am breathing—a helpless child,
a fragment in an adult game,
forgotten in an adult world…

Do you know me?

Do You Know Me?

Existence

A decade of "past" rushed
into a whirlpool of thousands of circles
with clearness of yesterday,

and I,

dizzy and lost,
backed away
to the present moment...

and the moment stretched in slow-motion
into decades and decades of past

inside the present's blurry passage.

Existence

Freedom

In the face of ravishing sorrows,
through the race of gruesome nights,
and threatening tomorrows,
through the chains of despotic powers
and the deceitful facade of plotting towers,

bleeding,

stepping on the sharp knives of
devious,
sanctimonious,
fanatic powers

Freedom keeps walking…

Freedom keeps laughing…

Freedom

Home

Would she ever see the land
where red tulips grew?
Would she ever see again
those emerald slopes?

Would she ever see Bamyan Lake—
the liquid shimmering turquoise blue?
Where Buddha sculptures used to stare…
Those peaceful dear old stone pair…

And will the children be running
on clover-covered grounds,
starry-eyed,
grubbing,
holding
the utopian skirts of tomorrow…
laughing, laughing…?

Would she ever?
Could she ever?

Hush, hush,
you *grown-old*, wandering alien.

Oh, regrets of yesterday,
where are her hopes?
And you—pains of life-mares,
where are her sweet dreams?
The blind war has crushed all the tulips,
and inside the bloodstained ruins—
mourning,

the wind echoes—
weeping, weeping…

Old songs, empty space,
my reflection, and I—
white hair, puffy eyes—
whispering, whispering…
"Would I ever? Could I ever?"

Donia Gobar, MD, MPH

Hospital Room

The icicles of waiting moments melt soundlessly
inside the slow, advancing tides of time.
Repositioning her aching head
on the warmed, white pillow,
she looks at the peach-colored walls,
and the "Little Sweet Moments" sign,
while the "touch and pass" half words
test
the patience of a semiconscious mind.

Looming *question marks* play
Hide and Seek games,
with her slowly waking-up thoughts
in the silence of room 223,
piercing
her mind and
the strong odor of antiseptics.

She gazes at the
yellow and purple common flowers,
as the stripes of white plastic shade
let the light of Pittsburg's gray sky
peak inside room 223
in vertical lines,
where she has lost
a day of her life.

Hypocrisy

"Do not fight!" they command,
watching the upturned young faces,
"Trust us!" they demand.
While the secret doors open and shut,
before where weapons are put to test,
"Our weapons must be the best!"
They make it their quest.

"Be fair!" they declare
as children play,
"Tell the truth!" with care
they say.
Yet,
they, as adults,
may hide the facts every day,
unashamed, unafraid,
as they *play and play.*

"Share what is yours!"
they give orders
to the young–and to the weak.
"Not yours!" they claim
as they take
that of others,
fencing the new borders.

What for…?
O…what for?
They will regret
someday
at the gates of death—

someday
leaving this world—
someday,
with no power, with no wealth…
And the curtains will fall—someday,
revealing the face of *Hypocrisy*—
someday…

Hypocrisy

Invisible

The pain is back—
in the pit of her heart,
where not a soul can see,
this horribly empty house—
wherein pain stretches
its dull weight,
settling in,
testing
the limits of human strength.

The slow-burning heat,
dragging behind it,
the flattering, wounded bird—
once her heart,
once the okay feeling,
up,
up to her throat,
up to her eyes,
up to the back of her neck,
to the back of her shoulders,
where it lingers;
where it stands guard;
not to let
the fleeting moments of hope
enter her aching soul.

Only…now and then
a sob breaks
the silence of her bare, gray world,
and her forehead presses down
on her thin fingers,

like storm-bearing clouds
on fragile limbs of an uprooted tree.
The palm of her hand
finds her swollen eyelids.

Tears—hot and sad
run down,
and she does not know what to do.

The candle, still lemon yellow,
stays in the gray light of dusk

The long leaves of the forgotten plant,
thirsty,
droop down the old window.

The hungry, red-eyed baby—
no more crying,
now and then…moaning,
is still
tapping on his mother's thin shoulders…

The red-eyed mother, playing tough,
her chin—up,
her arms holding—
the hungry, cold treasure…

Both in dark—
the invisibles…

Invisible

Leaving

I look at her small, pale face.
Her black-pearl eyes,
lost in sadness—
on the verge of words and tears...
She is not crying.
Standing there, three feet tall,
in a blue checkered sundress,
her arms thin and tan,
her small feet, lost in her shoes—
no socks...
She is just looking.
I press her hand three times,
meaning, *I love you,*
and she two times,
meaning *me too.*
I look into her eyes,
as my tears burn their way...
Time forces the distance to stretch,
and I have to go,
"It is okay to cry, see? I do,"
I say,
her thin shoulders warm and still.
I know I have to go.
I say "goodbye" and "see you again..."
as I step away...backwards,
my hand waving,
as I pull my bags along,
through the security service gateway
disappearing, slowly,
she is just standing there,

next to grown-ups,
waving, slowly
her tiny hands reaching up,
as high as they can…
I can't see her face anymore.
But I know she is not crying…

Life

I look at her *one-day-old* face,
and
she pouches her rose-petal lips,
and blinks—
merely for a second,
and goes back to sleep,
unaware of this world…
in clouds of white sheets.

A strange tenderness rushes
over, into my heart,
and I feel like crying…
I close my eyes.

Unconscious of thoughts,
thoughts find their way
to my lips,
and unaware of sound and silence,
a *silent* tear burns,
and disappears in a sigh,

"Ah…life, it has begun.
      What will become of it?"

"Listen...Oh watch...
You—People of the Earth,
Watch!"

I am here to stay in this world,
In this vast no man's world—not yours, not mine.
I saw the bombs devastate the land where I used to play.
I saw the ghastly choppers invade where I used to stay.
I cried when they stomped their dirty paws upon humanity,
and when they crushed honor and honesty.
I walked on this world—not yours, not mine,
nor dead, nor alive—a sad silent twine,
letting the hurt bleed itself dry—no words, no sigh...
in this vast no man's world—not yours, not mine.

My tears burned in rage when they misused
the words *Faith, Religion, God,* and *Nation,*
their atrocities, their shameless perversions
reflecting—in innocent blood, in children's horrified gaze
hiding—in graves, in women's mute life—that horrible maze.
I cried when they insulted mothers and fathers,
and when crippled orphans wandered—in daze.
I wept bitterly when they robbed the dignity of my people,
and when they stole the name of my people,
invisible in this world—not yours, not mine.

And then the Nightmare crept, suffocating, ugly, insane—
covering the mouths of my people;
hiding the truth about my people;
speaking falsely about my people...*my* people?
And I screamed, "*No, this is not the truth!*"
I sobbed quietly when heroes died—unknown.

They will not see the people free.
They will not smile again; walk again on a land—free.
The nightmare continued spreading dastardly crimes
in this amazing world—not yours, not mine.

Listen…O watch…You—people of the earth, watch!
The war-worn human beings, stripped of dignity,
running away in rags and dirt—from the assisted thieves
towards the closed doors, behind which the world marches…

I did cry; I threw my small fists up in the sky, asking, "Why?"
And the nightmare continues, creeping—decreed to destroy.
But the people are here to stay in this world—
in this vast no-man's world—not yours, not mine.
And we will shout out the voiceless truth—about *people,*
about innocent people in this world—not yours not mine.

Nightmare

I dreamt having to leave
my birthplace,
disaster of war and persecution chasing me.
I dreamt landing on another land,
where people
wrote and spoke unlike me,
altered my name, without asking me
and labeled me, without knowing me
looking at my lifelong professional resume,
concluding:
"Not approved! It does not have our seals!"
and,
"Must begin again!"
I dreamt that I was
sweating, in closed-off rooms
cleaning, in strangers' homes
shelving, in dusty storage rooms
sobbing, in glassed-up, muted cubes
Surviving,
breathing,
walking,
where the paths never ended…
and where logic was terminally ill.

I dreamt I cried alone,
thinking of a lost life,
watching my documents,
the results of lifelong work,
burning up…

I woke up.
It was only a nightmare!
Or was it?

No Illusions

In the small room where
I used to ponder
over the young face,
smiling back in wonder,
inside the friendly mirror in my room,
from the magical world of mirrors;
a world colored in silence,
behind the thin sheet of a painted glass—
existing in nothingness…

Tempted I had been, in young eagerness,
to reach in—
and touch
what was unreachable,
what was untouchable—
the unknown secrets of other worlds
in a young girl's room—in Kabul.

Leaning against the picture-spotted wall,
I had traveled thousands of miles…
Pictures I had cut from *Post* and *Life*
and *Ariana*, and *Times*, and
pictures I had walked into,
to look for the stories of lives
behind the mute images—in hide,
pictures that were small silent windows—
open to other worlds, all in a row,
on the walls of my room—in Kabul…

Where midnights used to find
my small figure,

bending over old papers
or card-boards
making mute shapes come to life
with my pencils
or brush strokes,
while the smell of lilacs
in our yard
had saturated all my senses…

I had looked up
into a star-jeweled cobalt blue sky
above the guarding Asmaii mountain,
wondering…
what was it like–
the world's other side?

Where nights,
I would look up
at two blinking red lights,
far away…

Where universe was embracing me,
on the rooftop of our three-story house;
the cool breeze caressing my young face,
wrapping my slim body in a white cotton dress;
and the millions and millions of stars dancing
in the magnificent deep blue space…

And I would return to my small room, amazed,
where medical books, bed, and bones
occupied all the space,
at the corner of rooftop of our house;
Where I would sit to continue learning
names of hundreds of vessels and nerves—

in the pages of Anatomy Gray,
and skeletal bones in the wooden box,
under my bed—in Kabul

Now, years later—
on the world's other side
I sit back, patiently,
for a moment…at my desk
Looking
at the young faces in a special school
At Cherokee Village—
Where I teach
hundreds of the mind's secrets,
in a small classroom,
where windows are shut.
and I think,
looking at the young faces—
from the world's other side,
with no illusions, no wonders!

Once Broken

She scribbled on the yellow page,
the color of seven falls on her face,
"The friendship is a puzzle;
    I look for the pieces;
        where did the friendship go?"

I remember,
those words, that small face,
those questioning brown eyes,
and my simple phrase:

    "It is going to be okay!"

And a light kiss,
a warm embrace…

And now,
a silent sadness…
Sitting quietly in the kitchen,
breeze-like, yellow curtains
between me and
the tree-lined gray sky.

Looking at the bare oak trees,
far away traveling geese,
rain washed brown leaves
matted on the patio,
and the empty street
on a Thanksgiving day…

I scribble on my mind,
the color of many falls
on my face,

"The friendships are puzzles;
    I look for the pieces;
        where did the friendship go?"

Silence breaths.
Occasional sizzling in the hot oven,
and the blowing sound
of the heat pump.
Not a small hug,
not even a light kiss.

It is not going to be okay!
Those deceptive patched cracks
are here to stay…

Overboard

I turn around, to see—
or not to see?
their small faces,
their eyes,
in the silence of their cries;

or not to hear?
their soundless whispers…,

"How it would feel,
if I could talk?
How it would feel,
if I could walk?
How it would feel,
when it is warm?
How it feels,
when there is no fear
and no pain?
How it feels
when one is loved?"

Not knowing, not asking.

They are the children—
overboard;
no rescue boats,
no rescue rings,
in the rushing market of life.

Soundless, pleads my soul to me.
Breathless, I close my eyes—
not to see…

not to hear…
in this dark winter night…
As we shudder—
my soul and me…

Overboard

Remember?

On the uneven sidewalks,
where the spring storm had left
unreachable tri-dimensional facts
in shallow layers of simple puddles.
And the aroma of jasmine flowers
made you dizzy,
looking…
down into the other deep blue sky,
lined by green coat oak guards,
standing
on the uneven stone sidewalks,
where your lace-tied braids
flew sideways,
while you,
jumped
over the many storm puddles,
pondering,
for just a moment, or more,
with the skip of a halfhearted beat,
looking
down
into the sky world of the puddles—
under your young quick feet,
jumping,
where you had picked armfuls of lilacs,
walking
on the uneven sidewalks.

Remember

Runaway

"Think future," I say to myself,
stepping over the present,
looking at the past,
pretending,

"No more hurting,
    no more remembering,
        only a faraway look…"

Shadow of a smile;
blinking away the tears;
not even a sigh…

The blurred vision of a ship—sinking.
A painful bruise throbbing
in my chest.

"Turn to the present," I say to myself
It is cold.
It is dark.
I hold onto the warm memories,
still
lighting my way,
softly…

"Will you light
someone's way
someday?"
I whisper to myself,
"A runaway?"

Runaway

Stars Are Raining

When in the poppy fields
of people's lives
cruel nights
were planting
the black flowers of sorrow;
and when
from dark eyes of the sky
sad stars were raining,
we were there…

When I saw
in silence of your eyes
the shaded river of human cries;
and when
on the thirsty meadow of a soul
your sad voice was raining,
we were there…

When
in the haven of night's deep forest,
in the path of brave knights,
diamonds of trust shimmered;
and when
with passing time
rain washed
the emeralds of the mind,
and
the periwinkle *forget-me-nots,*

from the fields of memories
were rising

We were there…

And when
the crushing cascade of life,
over the rebellious heroes rushed,
and the image of freedom was carved,
We were there…

Now,
away from those fall-colored eyes,
in the flood-ridden valley of a heart
red flower of sorrow
is growing,
and from the dark skies
of thousand-tongue silent eyes
tear-washed stars are raining,

I am here.

Swings

The old car breathes the last,
and I walk away
on the searing, cracked driveway.

The looming branches
watch
the lonely front yard,
and the wrinkled arm of an old oak
is holding
a pair of swings—
hanging side by side.

The earth has settled into cracks,
where the coal miners' bony fingers
reach out
from the pit-land of the past
ripping the old green outdoor mask.

I look at the swings,
the forgotten doors to the past.

I had wrapped vines and roses
around the yellow ropes,
remembering the wind,
bare feet, and green slopes…

Pale and tired, she was,
sitting on her luggage
between the past
and
the future passage.

My heart was pressed
inside some invisible fist.

Ah…laughter, laughter,
love and joy forever after…

Alas…time ran fast, leaving me
with the past;
and the swings are hiding
inside a sad, lonely dusk.

I enter a dark, empty corridor
And close behind me
the old green door.

Swings

The Café

Sounds of laughter and chatter
in the K. Pass Café in Parsons;
Kansas sky, hovering over
whispering secrets, fast cars,
and rushing walkers,
outside, in the small town.

Bob Dylan's voice scatters
verses,
as the words are blowing
in the wind,
as the ceiling fan stutters
inside…
As my pen stumbles
over
the paper napkins in haste,
"How was it then?"
Young age, all-night student café,
and Michigan snow—sleeping
outside…
"Future?" I had wondered then,
my bed waiting—untouched,
in the simple studio in Towers,
next to books and books…
A tired smile had softy rested
on my young face—then…

That *future* is the past—now…
My past—a treasure…?

And tomorrow—no more a mystery.

My bed, old and soft, waiting
in a simple old house,
on a country road…
Books, handwritten sheets,
canvases, and color-soaked brushes…
And a calm smile…has rested
on my seasoned face—now.

The Beautiful World

If only we all
were truly kind,
and knew empathy.

If only we all
did never lie,
and knew honesty.

If only we all
did not hurt others,
and knew sympathy.

If greed was used
to help,
and seek humanity.

If invention was for
keeping peace,
love, and equality.

If honor and dignity,
were people's
expected traits.

If we worked to live
and did *not*
live to work—for wealth.

If "the Earth"
meant
our Country.

If "human beings"
    meant
      our Nation

And if "the law of life"
    meant
        justice for humanity

Then…*O then,*
    this would be a
        a truly
            noble
                beautiful
                    world.

The Closing Doors

Look at those *runaway* eyes,
shutters—from earth to skies.
Listen to that empty voice,
"How is the weather?"
feelings, getting lost,
are running along
the quiet, dark back roads.

She walks in the soft, secure corridors,
in the everlasting land of her love,
in her wondering mind,
the place for those whom she loves…

Poor lashes struggle to keep
the warm, rushing flood in place.
She sees the closed door
with a name on it,
fading
in the dust of time—
unused,
forsaken for too long…
"Good," she says through the lumps,
through the overflowing flood,
"it has not been needed…"

She fights back
the tightness in her throat
and the tagging sentiment in her mind.
Defeated,
broken lashes nail shut the forgotten door…

Salty waters wash away the faded letters,
as she walks away,
farther and farther
from the door with no name on it.

The Last Season

The old woman in the white hospital bed
looked around the crowded room
in a nursing home,
as an old sweeper, sweeping
the fallen leaves off a neglected tomb.
Her lost look, keeping guard,
a mixture of gray and white worry
in a vacuum of unknowingness,
dipping in and out of the wells of sight.
The pale cream wrinkled fingers
weak and bony,
persistent,
trudged along to get
the rectangular ivory object,
with the call button on it—
the lifeline for the bedridden patient,
innocently left—
just a little out of reach
for the exhausted hand to reach.

The old woman held her breath
to cross the bridge
of pain
in her back,
thinking of a dry twig—
snap—
resting against the white angular fence,
when her children had jumped
yesterday?
—Or last century?...

Discerned with an automatic smile,
the crisp-white-uniformed helper's face
came close to the old timid face,
while the efficient hands
repositioned the pillows and the brace.
This face was not that of her child,
whose tears she had kissed away…
moments before?
Or was it years before?
The cream-colored door fell in place,
as the young nurse left the room,
blocking the path
of the sad, following gaze…
As the alphabet blocks she had made,
had fallen in her children's room
as the summer-blue door
had closed
behind the young mother
leaving the room…
moments ago?
—or was it years ago?

The old, lost look swept the empty space,
a mixture of gray and white worry
in a white, half-asleep resting home.

The Mute Shore In Me

Look at those rushing, young emotions,
racing with children of the sea,
scattering diamonds of illusion.

Tipsy, with the wine of crimson dusk,
rising, falling,
and with half-breed twilights,
crying,
and with the mystic blue moon
singing, dancing…

Again and again and again

The old shore in me watches
silently,
stretching out its world-weary being,
its vulnerable soft edges,
slowly
breaking,
sinking,
where the young waves play
night after night,
day after day…

The Portrait In Ink

Outside,
in the stone-paved hallway
words and sentences—halfway
and children's step—getting away
and adults' pace
echo—my way.

Inside,
from the old school desk,
through the ink lines I make
on the legal pad's page
the questioning gaze
in the young boy's face
stares back in a daze.

Will he make it
—through the storms?
Will he survive
—through the norms?
In the world of foster homes
and juvenile courts.

Another lost young soul.
Another silent plea.
Another sad goodbye.

The portrait in ink,
now, folded in four—is gone,
with the yellow school bus,
and the pale-faced boy,
and the hand—waving at me…

The Teacher

I am a simple person
    Color blind
    Gender blind
    Religion blind
    Borders blind

I am a learner
    Always
    Alert
    Unafraid
    Amazed

I am a follower
    Of simple logic
    Simple heroes
    Tested wisdom
    True freedom

I am a leader
    Patient
    Sincere
    Fair
    Aware

I am a healer
    Color blind
    Gender blind
    Religion blind
    Border blind

I am "*Me*"
　　Like everyone
　　Like no one…

Donia Gobar, MD, MPH

The Ugly Face of Power

They all shine,
sinking in soft velvet seats,
where ruby-colored drapes
mark the theater.

we all watch,
in the face of undeniable reality
the dissolving process of the "*Nobodies*"
whose lips
have not touched the tips
of *golden skirts;*
whose hands
have not polished *spotted shoes*
of *"somebodies"*—
in the murky halls of power.

We all sigh,
hearing the sound of imitated wisdom,
as twisted images fall into the mosaic
of popular subjects;
as hollow ideas bubble out
of a suffocated marshland,
where the bodies of truth and wisdom
have been slaughtered
and abandoned.

My thoughts—
the misplaced peaceful observers
struggle in dark,
as the *lefts* and *rights* lie in wait,
camouflaged,

in the battlefield of contradictions,
to entrap
the scattered feverish emotions;
and,
as the distinct smell of rotted facts
marks the unmarked marshlands,
quietly, we house
the wounded images of the intellect
and of the innocent
in the concentration fields of survivors;
so that the great ugly powers may not ridicule
the hunchbacked carriers of freedom,
as we gasp for truth
at the edges of unmarked marshlands
in the battlefield of our lives.

Donia Gobar, MD, MPH

They Can't Take Freedom From Me

Do not pity me!
Think of me!
I won't let them take freedom from me.
Just a child I am, look at me!
Only a child, remember?
Superpower is passing through.
Remember!
The invader's shrewd and shameless,
calculated crimes
have made a masterpiece out of me.

Look at me!

My eyes used to sparkle with smiles.
My hands, while I still had them,
were soft and skilled.
I could run, my feet swift—like you.
I could jump and dance—like you.
I could see and laugh—like you.

Look at me!

It was a doll—a present from invaders.
Unlike Trojan horse,
this one had explosives
for children—like me.

Now,
I am not the child I used to be.
Go and tell the world,
"Remember!
　　　Here are millions of *masterpieces*—

just like me;
the background—no more green,
no more alive,
is signed in blood—
                    Invaders"

Remember me, as my silent vow
echoes
in Afghanistan valleys,
        "They can't take freedom from me."
        "They can't take freedom from me."

Untouched

Let me close my eyes
and forget
the hand of mankind—
changing
the giving earth,
the amazing earth,
into
a pierced,
battered,
stabbed
abstract.

Oh, let me remember,
to see,
for a moment,
and
to never
forget
the patient
marvelous
earth—
untouched.

Voyager

Ye' life, show me your cards;
empty hands do not scare me anymore.

And you—the winding roads ahead,
your slippery twists and turns
do not weary me anymore.

O darkness!
Show me the darkest of sights,
and the creepiest of nights!
My heart does not
race in fear anymore.

And you, the cowardly powers of hypocrisy,
your calculated and evil harmony,
your fierce dark symphony,
and the slippery, shapeless nature
of your two-faced face
do not deceive me anymore.

And ah, disaster,
your unpredictable *hit and run* cruelty
does not astonish me anymore;
and your raving, blindfolded tyranny
does not stop me anymore...

But oh, you—memories from the past,
and hopes of tomorrow
rain on me, softly, softly!
You are the only pleasures I would ask for,
more and more...

Voyager

War

Did you see?
Did you?
The lifeless limbs, the limbless lives,
and the bloody curls
around pain-struck faces...

Did you hear?
Did you?
The voiceless screams,
bewildered
in the pause of rushing time...

Did you shudder with rage?
Thinking of the cowards
watching the criminals
and their self-serving ideals...

Were you there?
Were you?
Watching the children's lives set
in chilling, bloody twilights of war

Alas, alas...
All those unspoken words...

Tell me, did you weep?
Did you ask?
"Why...
       why?"

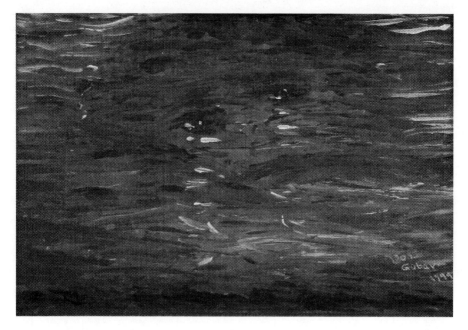

War

What Am I?

The long wooden table,
and
the mustard-colored old school—
somewhere in east coast land…

The weightless popcorn—scattered,
pale, forlorn,
waiting
to be picked
by all those fingers—
old and robust, or carefully manicured;
to disappear
beyond dried-up plums or soft cherries
of all those mouths
—one by one.

Hearing their easy flow of words—
a language not mine,
I walk away in my mind,
getting lost in strangers' shores…
Ah, rushing, crushing waves…
what am I?

Awake and alone in grave—
this airless tiny ditch
pressed down by life—
this blind weight.
A soundless scream
in long, dead-end roads.

Silently waiting, waiting
Watching, watching—
the senseless craze…

A painful wound—a flameless burn
A searching wave at invisible shores…

What am I?

My body—a stretcher for lives
My mind—a runaway soul
in nightmare corridors…
A rebellious slave—
chased in hateful dark halls?
Running, gasping—between closing walls.
Small-talk messengers holding
my eyelids open;
mute tears pounding at the pretence walls
"Yes," "No," and "Thanks," I say…

What am I?

Footsteps, once so small—
skipping, running, dancing
on the dust, on the mud,
on the asphalt roads
slowing down—
hushed in deep thoughts,
faraway—in college compasses,
on rented floors,
on hospital grounds, in my patients' rooms.
In sidewalk cafes,
in strangers' homes,

in old, musty classrooms
pacing…

What am I?

"Look down!
The mountains are getting lost;
tears leave; I will return at last."
I had watched then
I had said then

"Look! I can exist in them all—
the world around
the world inside,
the world away—miles and miles…"

I smile now,
a shrewd little smile…

Listen!
I can hush the cry's echo
in hollow nights…

See?
I look at the young green leaves,
and
touch so tenderly the yellow buttercups,
and dewdrops at dawn…

Yet,
raindrops in gray twilights
sadly pause,
and run on my soul,
and
I smile,

a shrewd little smile,
while it hurts, while it burns…

what am I?

What Am I?

Wishing…

Oh little, soft, magical snowflakes…
look at those shiny brown boots.
Look at the soft, furry white lining…
only one pair, just the size of my boots.

God, they must be real warm…
oh, how I could run—
on the muddy back alee,
and on the crisp icy snow,
in those brown, lovely, warm boots.

Oh, my nose, it is numb…
and freezing.
My pinky finger and my thumb
frozen in place…
and surely I don't feel my toes.
Well,
maybe tonight I will dream…
being warm
in those shiny rubber boots,
having in my arms
that doll
with the bonnet and the white boots.

Wishing

About the Author

Donia Gobar is the daughter of Salia Ghobar and M.G.M. Ghobar, the author of "Afghanistan in the Course of History." Born in Kabul, Afghanistan, she graduated from Kabul University, School of Medicine, specializing in Obstetrics and Gynecology. She continued her medical career in West Berlin, with a specialty in Internal Medicine. Dr. Gobar was awarded a Masters degree in Public Health from the University of Michigan, and conducted biomedical research at the University of Illinois. In addition, Dr. Gobar undertook the National Teachers Examination and went on to earn alternative teaching certificates for both Massachusetts and Kansas. Currently, she is an instructor and the creative force behind a curriculum called "Concept of Health." Her daughter is attending medical school in the US. Dr. Gobar's hobbies include painting, creative writing, and sculpting.

Dr. Gobar is the founder of the True Humanity Club (http://clubs.yahoo.com/clubs/Truehumanity). She is a member of National Education Association, KNEA—Human & Civil Rights Commission. She has also done several art exhibitions in places such as George Mason University (Society of Afghan Artists, 1999), Pittsburg Arts Council (1999, 2000, 2001, and 2003), and Fort Scott, Kansas (2000). While a medical student, when making a sculpture, her picture was selected to appear on the cover of *Overseas* magazine, as well as in *Scala* magazine. Some of her work can be viewed at www.geocities.com/dgobard/Donia.htm.

Dr. Gobar is listed as a literary writer in "The Encyclopedia of Persian Literature In Afghanistan." Her work includes "Aya," which was published in the "Top Ten Short Stories of 1994" (American Literary Press, Inc.), *Dunya-e-Jawanan*, and *Afghan Magazine* (Lemar-Aftaab). Other short stories of hers, written and published in Persian (Dari) language, have appeared in various magazines and newspapers in Kabul, Germany and Canada. She was awarded the *International Poet of Merit Award* in 2000-2001 and 2003. She has also received the *Editor's Choice Award*, and her work has been chosen for Poetry's Elite—*Best Poets of Year 2000* by the International Society of Poets (ISP). Her poems have been featured on ISP's "Sound of Poetry" CDs.

0-595-29303-4